PAGES

A Library Tale

by D. R. Sanchez

This is a work of fiction. Names, characters, businesses, places, events and incidents are either the products of the author's imagination or used in a fictitious manner. Any resemblance to actual persons, living or dead, or actual events is purely coincidental.

Copyright © 2016 by Debra R. Sanchez

All rights reserved. This book or any portion thereof may not be reproduced, performed or used in any manner whatsoever without the express written permission of the publisher or author except for the use of brief quotations in a book review.

Printed in the United States of America

First Printing 2016

ISBN 13: 9780692673904
ISBN10: 0692673903

Tree Shadow Press
www.treeshadowpress.com

For performance permission, contact:
Debra R. Sanchez
dbrsanchez@gmail.com

Cover art by Debra Sanchez. Author photo by Melissa Schneider.

Dedicated to all who inspired it.
Thank you to:

My parents and grandparents
for feeding my love of books and libraries.

My children and grandchildren
for keeping that love alive.

My mentors for teaching me
how to put words on a page.

All of the writing groups I have
belonged to or led over the years.

And especially to the libraries of my life, from
the first one that I rode my bike to every week
as a child in Mars, PA to the ones I was lucky
enough to work for as an adult.

Without libraries life is nothing.

Pages was first produced July 28, 2015 in Springdale, PA. A power point slide show, projected on a screen behind the actors on stage, was used as setting and background.

ORIGINAL CAST
(alphabetically by character name)

ALEX (adult)..Starr Bryson

ALEX (teen)...Britt Strand

LIBBY...Laura Welsh

LEXI...Kerry E. B. Black

NARRATOR............................... HanaHaatainen-Caye

PAIGE...Jenifer McNamara

PETER...Josh Seybert

TOM..Vic Robb

VOICE / STAGE MANAGER................Megan Vance

CHARACTERS:

NARRATOR Reads book or notebook in a comfortable chair either on the side of the stage, or behind audience.

ALEX Library Patron/Student (high school, then older) can be male or female. Adjust script pronouns as needed. Wears a lanyard or bulky necklace (or tie if male), which passes to **OLDER ALEX/NARRATOR** in final scene to show character identity.

LEXI Library Patron

LIBBY Librarian

PAIGE Assistant Librarian & mother of **ALEX**

PETER Friend of the Library

TOM Friend of the Library

SETTING:

Library Split stage. Library Circulation Desk on one side with a phone. Comfortable chair on the other. Bookshelves near desk. Can also be played with the **NARRATOR** chair located behind the audience.

SYNOPSIS OF SCENES

SCENE ONE
In a small community library, present.

SCENE TWO
Same, another day.

SCENE THREE
Same library, several years later.

SCENE FOUR
Outside the library, three years later.

SCENE FIVE
Empty lot, one year later.

SCENE SIX
Abandoned parking lot, three years later.

SCENE SEVEN
Several years late

PAGES

Scene 1

At Rise:

NARRATOR *is seated in comfortable chair, with open book/notebook.* **LIBBY** *and* **PAIGE** *are busy at the desk. The phone rings.*

LIBBY. Good afternoon, Town Library, Libby speaking.
(Pause. Looks at watch or clock)
It's 12:34.
(Pause)
You're welcome.
(Hangs up phone, then speaks to **PAIGE***)*
Honestly, Paige, the way some people abuse us. If you're going to call the library for information, well, not you, but people, you know what I mean. If you're going to call for information, make it worth answering.

PAIGE. Remember the time that person called to ask how to spell Katy? Impossible to know. Do they mean with a "C" or a "K"? Ending with "I"? "IE"? "Y"? Please.

LIBBY. Or those people who wanted to find out where they should call for chicken delivery.

PAIGE. Three times in one day.

LEXI. *(Approaches desk)*
Could one of you help me?

LIBBY. Of course, that's why we're here.

LEXI. I'm looking for information about the history of libraries. But I also need to find out about electronic libraries.

PAGES

PAIGE. A good place to start is in the catalog, especially if you want books. It used to be that the only way to get that kind of information was from the card catalog. A few libraries still use that along with the current system.

LEXI. Current? You mean on the computer, right?

PAIGE. Yes. The computerized library produces better results than the card system, faster too. It's still good to understand how the card catalog works in case the computers are down for any reason. Come with me, I'll show you how to use it.

(LEXI follows PAIGE to a computer as PAIGE guides her through the steps. Phone rings and LIBBY answers.)

LIBBY. Good afternoon, Town Library, Libby speaking.
(Pause)
Let me see if I understood what you asked. You want information about Tacoma in the state of Warsaw? Did you mean Washington?
(Pause)
But, sir, Are you sure? Warsaw is not a state. Washington is.
(Pause followed by a startled motion. LIBBY continues, to audience.)
He hung up on me. *(Sigh)*

(As NARRATOR speaks, PAIGE and LEXI exit behind bookshelves.)

NARRATOR. I remember how it was. When I was little, my mother worked in the library. Story time was my favorite. I always had piles of books. From the library, mostly, but also stacks and stacks of my own books.

When I learned to read, my obsession with books blossomed.

PAGES

I had my own library card and made full use of the school's library, too, unlike some of the other kids who only went when a teacher insisted on a book report.

You know something? Book reports were hard for me, too. Not because I didn't want to do them. I had trouble deciding which book to pick. How can you pick just one?

After a while, there wasn't much left in the school library. That made it was hard to find anything that I hadn't already read.

Scene 2

*(**ALEX** enters and approaches desk, carrying a stack of books.)*

LIBBY. Hi Alex.

ALEX. Mom's off today, but I couldn't wait to pick up those books that came in for me.

LIBBY. Paige works again tomorrow, you couldn't wait one more day?

ALEX. No. I couldn't. I love that I can still get books here. The school's library doesn't have anything for me anymore.

LIBBY. The way you read, it's a wonder any library can keep up.

ALEX. At least this library still tries. The one at school keeps losing books.

LIBBY. Losing books?

ALEX. That's what they say anyway. But I've been paying attention. They are eliminating books, especially any that I might be interested in. Some of the best books I've ever read…gone.

LIBBY. Oh. *(Beat)* That. *(Beat)* I knew it was happening in many places, but I didn't realize it was happening here.

ALEX. They've eliminated some books that used to be required reading, like *To Kill a Mockingbird, The Catcher in the Rye, The Giver,* even really old ones like *The Adventures of Huckleberry Finn.* And silly books like *Where's Waldo*…gone.

PAGES

(Pause)
I'm glad I don't have to worry about losing books here.

LIBBY. *(Looks around before speaking)*
Not yet, anyway.

ALEX. What do you mean, "Not yet, anyway?"

LIBBY. Libraries across the country are facing serious financial troubles. Many end up being shut down because they can't afford to stay open. Some only continue thanks to the efforts of volunteers. We've come to depend more and more on the donations and help we get from community members.

ALEX. Like "Friends of the Library?" Mom says they help a lot.

LIBBY. Exactly. Paige and I, and the other library staff, need all the help we can get to keep the library running.

*(As they speak **LIBBY** checks out the books for **ALEX**)*

ALEX. What happens if people stop supporting the library?

LIBBY. Well, we would have to depend completely on government funding, and that budget shrinks every year. It would mean not being able to buy new books, or replace older ones when they are worn out. And, of course, we'd have to have a smaller staff, and possibly close the library or drastically reduce hours.

ALEX. That sounds terrible. What would I do for books? My family can't afford to buy all the books I want to read.

LIBBY. I doubt any family could afford to keep you in books, Alex.

LIBBY(cont).
(Chuckles)
It's people like you who need libraries. Libraries need people like you. In fact, the world needs people like you. People who care about reading. The more you read, the more you think, and the more you think, the more likely you are to find solutions to problems.

ALEX. So, you're saying that my love of reading will save the world someday?

LIBBY. *(Closes last book in the check-out stack)*
That's not quite what I said. But, you never know…it could.

ALEX. *(Picking up the books)*
You never know…it just might.

*(Phone rings, **LIBBY** answers)*

LIBBY. Good afternoon, Town Library, Libby speaking.
(Pause. Looks at watch or clock)
It's 5:05.
(Pause)
You're welcome.
(Hangs up phone, then speaks to Audience)
Some things never change.

ALEX. *(Turns to leave)*
I'll see you next week.

LIBBY. See you then.

*(**ALEX** exits)*

PAGES

NARRATOR. As I grew older, I hate to admit it, but I let my life keep me away from the library more and more. I was too busy with sports and music and developing a social life. I barely had time to keep up with school assignments, and much less time for reading for my own enjoyment.

I often managed to sneak in "reading for pleasure" time instead of doing homework…or sleeping. Reading is like a drug. Sometimes, you just need a fix.

Then I got my first Kindle. I loaded it up with all of my favorites and took it with me for when I had a few minutes to read. I stopped making time to go to the library. Why bother when for a few bucks you could download the book you wanted…without the trip to the library…or store…or the wait for delivery of the books I used to buy online…I did miss the library, though.

Really. I did.

After college, I went to graduate school to get my MLS. That's a Master's degree in Library Science, in case you were wondering. I didn't finish. The outlook was too bleak.

PAGES

Scene 3

Library, several years later. **LIBBY** *is putting books into boxes throughout the scene.* **PETER** *and* **TOM** *enter with empty boxes.*

PETER. We brought you more boxes, like you asked. Will you need many more?

LIBBY. Of course. LOTS more. As many as you can find.

TOM. Peter said that you needed help with moving stuff to temporary storage. Why isn't the library giving you the boxes?

LIBBY. Shhh…
(Looks around)
I thought I could trust you two. Peter, didn't you tell him what's happening?

PETER. No, I didn't. I was worried he'd say something before we got here. And I thought it would be better if you told him. You know my memory stinks.

LIBBY. That's true. Your memory's so full of holes it might as well be Swiss cheese. Tom, here's the problem. The library has been ordered to remove certain books from the shelves.

The town's new censoring committee has decided that it's dangerous for the public to be allowed to read any book that has been on the "Top 100 Banned and/or Challenged Books" list going all the way back to 1990. Lots of them were on the list for several years, but still…that's a LOT of books. And most of those books are important.

They want me to just toss them all into the incinerator, but there's no way I can do that. So, we're packing them up and putting them some place where they'll be safe.

It makes me sick to think of being forced to destroy any book just because some people might be offended. At least the library will remain open. And there are plenty of other books that haven't hit that list...at least not yet.

*(Enter **ALEX**)*

ALEX. Are we late?

LIBBY. No. Not really. I'm just glad you could make it. Where did you park?

ALEX. I put the truck out back, like you asked. Mom's on her way in. She's driving her car so that we could get more out tonight.

LIBBY. Good. Peter, Tom start taking these out. Is the truck locked?

ALEX. *(Nods)*
Here's the key.
*(Hands key to **PETER**)*
I found a great place, too.

LIBBY. To park? The lot should have been almost empty since it's almost time to close.

*(**PETER** and **TOM** exit with full boxes.)*

ALEX. No, to put the books. I've got tons of shelves and everything. I'm taking them to...

PAGES

LIBBY. *(Interrupting)*
NO…don't tell me. It's best if I don't know, just in case.

ALEX. In case what?

LIBBY. Come on, Alex. You're smart. You know what I mean.

ALEX. Oh. Yeah. That.

LIBBY. Yeah. That.

*(**PAIGE** enters carrying empty boxes.)*

PAIGE. Hi Libby.

LIBBY. Hi. How have you been? Since they let you go, I never get to see you anymore.

PAIGE. I've been ok. Alex helps me out a lot. I miss being here, but the bus stopped going near our house, and I can't justify spending the money for gas just to visit.

LIBBY. I can't believe how expensive it is now.

*(**PAIGE** helps **LIBBY** pack books into boxes.)*

ALEX. I guess it's a good thing I quit library school. I hate my job, but at least it pays enough to let me fill up the tank once in a while.

LIBBY. You would've been an amazing librarian. We're a dying breed.
*(Phone rings, **LIBBY** answers)*
Good evening, Town Library, Libby speaking.

(Pause. Looks at watch or clock)
It's 7:45. We close at 8:00.
(Pause)
You're welcome.
(Hangs up phone, then speaks to Audience)
Honestly. Can you believe it?

(PETER *and* **TOM** *return,* **LIBBY** *and* **PAIGE** *continue to fill boxes.)*

PETER. Are there many more?

LIBBY. Yes, but we'll have to finish another day. We have to be out of here by closing time. The lights go out 5 minutes after, and it's impossible to see anything. And they have some new-fangled security system that doesn't need electricity, and I can't open the doors once the power is off.

TOM. *(Picks up a box.)*
How bizarre.

LIBBY. Like one of those science fiction books you have in there.
(LIBBY *motions to the others and the boxes.)*
OK, the three of you better get these on the truck before I have to lock up. Paige, you and I can take these last boxes.

(ALEX, PETER *and* **TOM** *exit with boxes.)*

PAIGE. I'll take these tote bags, too. I think I can carry some with a box.
(Starts to pick up a box.)

LIBBY. Wait.

PAGES

*(**PAIGE** pauses, looking at **LIBBY**)*

PAIGE. I thought you said we had to hurry.

LIBBY. We do, but I don't know when I'll see you again. I didn't get to thank you for all the years you worked with me.
(Takes a deep breath)
I don't know what might happen if they find out what we've done, and I want you to know how much your help means to me, both back in the day, and even more now.

PAIGE. I'll be back. You know that. Once the economy recovers, they'll need me back.

LIBBY. I wish. They stopped buying books. They say people don't need actual books anymore since they are available so easily on e-readers.
(Begins to tear up and fights back the tears.)
I wonder how long it will be before they eliminate me, too. They've already reduced library hours to two hours on weekday evenings, and eight hours on Saturdays.

PAIGE. *(Pats **LIBBY**'s arm, then gives her a hug/pat on the back for reassurance.)*
Never give up hope.
(Glances at watch/clock.)
Come on now. It's almost time. We wouldn't want to be locked in the library until Monday evening, now, would we? You want a ride? I'd be happy to take you home.

LIBBY. You're right, it's late. I planned to walk home, but I'd love a ride.
(Wipes tears)

PAGES

Let's go.

*(**PAIGE** puts a tote bag full of books on each arm, picks up a box, and exits. **LIBBY** gets her purse and picks up another box, looks around the room, sighs and exits.)*

(Offstage)

VOICE. STOP! Police! Put down those boxes.

LIBBY. It's ok. I work here.

VOICE. I said drop them! *(Beat)* Now!

(Sounds of a scuffle and taser)

PAIGE. *(Screams)*

NARRATOR. Things don't always work out as planned. Sometimes people succeed. Other times, plans are blown to bits.

Over the years, a few underground libraries were set up in various parts of the country. Some remain hidden. Some were found and destroyed. Some never stood a chance. I've heard that some were set up, but the people who established them disappeared and were never heard from again. Those collections remain lost to this day.

*(As **NARRATOR** speaks, set up next scene. Put up the chains and padlock.)*

Scene 4

Outside library. Three years later. A padlock on chains is visible over a door or opening representing a door. **TOM, LEXI, PETER** *meet near entrance.*

TOM. Are you sure Alex is coming?

PETER. Of course. Why wouldn't s/he?

TOM. You know. Because of what happened.

LEXI. Oh, Tom. You obviously don't know Alex like we do. It is BECAUSE of what happened that you KNOW s/he'll be here.

PETER. Remember when Paige introduced us, Lexi?

LEXI. Best thing that ever happened to me.

PETER. Me too.

LEXI. It wasn't long after she taught me how to use the library.

PETER. And she had you help me learn. Those were the days.

LEXI. I just wish I could have been here THAT day. Maybe if I had been things would have worked out.

PETER. You can't blame yourself. As they say in Spanish, "Lo hecho, hecho esta." What's done, is done. Besides, maybe if we had waited a little longer, or…

TOM. If we'd waited any longer, they'd've caught us, too. Look, here comes Alex.

PAGES

*(**ALEX** approaches, pulling a key on a lanyard from a pocket, looking around before speaking.)*

ALEX. I got it. Let's do this.

TOM. You ok?

ALEX. I'm fine. I'll never get over it, but I can sleep. I can eat.

LEXI. The library's been closed for three years, now, ever since…well…you know.

ALEX. *(Sighs)*
Yeah, I know.

PETER. I'm just glad that they've disconnected that crazy security system.

ALEX. I can't believe Libby was able to let me know where to find a key. I don't know how she found out about it. Maybe one of the guards has a soft place in their heart for books or something.

TOM. Or, it could be a trap.

LEXI. *(Nodding)*
It could, you know.

ALEX. That's why we have to get in and out as fast as we can. I've been in contact with other people like us. I have real hope that what we're doing will succeed. It has to or Mom's…

*(Falls silent. **LEXI** hugs **ALEX**.)*

LEXI. Come on. Let's get in and out before anyone shows up. Your mom would've wanted you to be careful.

ALEX. I'm still FURIOUS at them for killing her.

TOM. They said it was an accident.

PETER. Come on, Tom, you know they didn't have to taser her at all. They killed her, plain and simple.

TOM. I was just saying that they didn't mean to kill her. They didn't know she'd have a heart attack from it.

PETER. It doesn't matter if they meant to or not…they did it. Let's go. We owe it to Paige.

ALEX. And to Libby, too. Maybe I can get a book to her next time I visit her in prison.

*(**ALEX** opens the lock, removes the chain, and one by one they go in, and come out with boxes, tote bags, etc. **ALEX** is the last one to return, and relocks the chains.)*

ALEX. Ok. Next week. Same time, right? Let's get out of here before they show up.

ALL. *(Overlapping variations as they go their separate ways)*
Bye. Til next week. Be careful.

*(As **NARRATOR** speaks, remove chains and padlock.)*

PAGES

NARRATOR. Eventually all libraries lost patrons, lost funding and were closed down...for good. Well, not for *good* but forever. Some of them were left standing, especially in towns where books held a special place in the hearts of the community. But, many more were demolished. For the most part, demolition crews salvaged nothing.

The reason? My guess is corporate greed. Isn't that why most things happen in this world? The reason the officials gave was that books and libraries were no longer needed. Everything that anyone might need was readily available in digital form. And whatever you couldn't find online...well...that was information *you* didn't need.

Who cared about old manuscripts and documents? They were part of the past, and the past was gone and done with. People were supposed to focus on the future, to think of how many trees would be saved by eliminating the use of paper altogether.

Hhhmmph. Right. Save the trees. Sure. They plowed down countless acres of forest to gain city space, the same way they paved over libraries...for more parking lots.

PAGES

Scene 5

One year later. **ALEX, TOM, LEXI** *and* **PETER** *meet where the chains and padlock had been, now an empty pile of dirt and rubble.*

ALEX. *(Visibly upset. Using arms for emphasis.)*
THIS IS INSANE!

LEXI. *(Crying)*
I can't believe it. It's gone!

PETER. *(Places arm over **LEXI**'s shoulder to comfort her.)*
The dust hasn't settled yet. There might still be someone around.

ALEX. There's no one here. Look. Nothing but FLAT DESTRUCTION! Not even a stray book. Nothing. There's NOTHING LEFT!

TOM. Alex is right, Peter. There's no one here.

ALEX. I should've made more trips. I should've come every day, not every week. We still had so many to save.

PETER. You know that wouldn't have been possible. You know we've been pushing our luck with coming every week this last year. It's a miracle we've been able to get gasoline…and a bigger miracle that we weren't caught.

LEXI. *(Shrugging **PETER**'s arm off her shoulder.)*
It's almost a good thing that Libby didn't live to see this. Paige, too. At least Libby died knowing that we were doing everything in our power to save the books.

PAGES

ALEX. Yeah, but she suspected this was going to happen sooner or later. She managed to keep those books I took her hidden, right up 'til the end. She was holding one when she died.

TOM. Which book was it?

ALEX. Which one do you think it was?

TOM. Oh. I think I know…was it…?

(Pauses with a raised eyebrow. Raises fingers to show the numbers 4, 5, 1.)

ALEX. Yes, that one.

LEXI. Now what?

ALEX. Now what, what?

LEXI. Now what do we do? We can't get any more books out. Not without a shovel.

TOM. None of them would be readable after that.
(Points to rubble.)

PETER. That's for sure. So
*(Turns to **ALEX**)*
What IS next?

ALEX. Why are you all asking me? Who made me leader?

PETER. Who else? You've been behind our actions for years now. It was your idea to start saving the challenged and banned books before the library was in real danger.

ALEX. Oh…yeah…and what a *great* idea that was. That *brilliant* plan landed Libby in jail and KILLED my mom.

PETER. Still. It really was a great idea. It's not your fault it took that terrible twist. You found a place to keep the books. You've dedicated your LIFE to this. And, we're with you. One hundred percent. *(Beat)* At least I am. You guys?

LEXI. Of course. You know I'll do anything you say, Alex.

TOM. Me too.

ALEX. I need to get away from all this. It might be a good idea if we don't do anything for a while. I was planning to tell you all that tonight was the last night. For me anyway. I feel like I'm being watched, especially since Libby passed away.

LEXI. We can't just give up.

ALEX. I didn't say give up. I just meant…I don't know…take a break?

PETER. I've noticed some people who seem to be watching me, too, but I just figured I was getting paranoid.

TOM. I was wondering how I'd be able to tell you guys that I needed out. My boss has been paying extra attention to my emails and we've had several gasoline inventories lately. I'm scared they'll find out that I've been skimming it for these runs.

ALEX. It almost seems like the end of our library, as tragic and horrible as it really is, might have been a blessing in disguise.

PAGES

*(***LEXI**, **PETER** *and* **TOM** *reluctantly nod in agreement.)*

ALEX. So. *(Beat)* This is it. For now anyway. Let's plan to meet back here…no matter what…in…I don't know…three years? No matter what, three years from today at this time.

*(***LEXI**, **PETER** *and* **TOM** *nod again. All four hug each other goodbye and go their separate ways.)*

NARRATOR. It's hard to imagine a world without libraries.
Even harder to imagine a world without books.

Scene 6

Three years later
No one on stage. Quiet for 15 seconds, then enter **LEXI**.

LEXI. *(Aloud, to self.)*
Looks like I'm the first one here.
(Pause.)
I wonder if anyone else will show up.

(Quiet for 15 seconds, then enter **TOM***)*

TOM. *(Brief embrace/shoulder pat/etc.)*
Lexi, you're here. I wondered if you'd make it. Have you heard from the others?

LEXI. Haven't heard from Alex since the last time. I saw Peter a few weeks ago. He said he planned on coming…if he could figure out how to get here.
(Looks around nervously.)
How long should we wait?

TOM. I'd give them a while still.

(Awkward silence for 15 seconds, then enter **PETER***.)*

TOM. You made it.

PETER. *(Briefly embraces* **TOM** *and* **LEXI***.)*
It wasn't easy. Where's Alex?

LEXI. S/he's not here yet.

PAGES

(Awkward silence for 5 seconds.)

PETER. Did you guys see on TV what's happening to the e-book industry?

TOM. I didn't. I can't afford television anymore. Phone either. I do still have my computer, but when it quits…I'm done.

LEXI. You mean the way they're making people pay higher fees to keep the e-books on their devices?

PETER. Yeah. That's what I meant. That's crazy. They convince people to dump all their books, and then….

TOM. They didn't *convince* me.

LEXI. Me either.

PETER. They get *most* people to dump all their books and go all digital, then WHAM! Make them pay more for it.

LEXI. I heard that they have a legal right to do it because all those books people bought for their electronic readers don't belong to them, even though they *bought* them.

TOM. That was the problem with those things all along. I saw that coming since the beginning. If you read the fine print, you see that with e-books, you do not own the material. You only own temporary rights to read the material and to have it in your possession. You can't lend it or sell it. I wondered when corporate greed was going to step in and start extorting people who want to have written material to read. That's why I stashed my own books away while we were saving the library books.

PAGES

PETER. I hope you have them well hidden. Don't you live in an apartment? The new city ordinances prohibit book owning as a fire hazard.

TOM. No, I moved out of that apartment right after the last time we were here. I'm actually living way out...not far from where we put...you know...
(looks around and lowers voice)
the books. That way I've been able to keep an eye on things. I've got plenty of room, if either of you ever need to get out of here.

LEXI. That's good to know. I've been wondering how to deal with all that's been going on lately. I lost my job and am about to lose my apartment. I've been selling my things just to buy food. But, not my books. And, I really need to get those out before the fire marshal does the next inspection.

TOM. Let me give you directions. I'd give you the address, but I don't want anyone to Google it. I've managed to stay off the grid since going out there.

PETER. But, you said you still used your computer.

TOM. Yes, I do use the computer...but I'm not using internet. I use it for my writing. I'm counting on the day when books will be important again. That day has to come.

PETER. I'm sure it will. Lexi, how will you get your stuff out to Tom's place?...If that's what you plan to do now.

LEXI. I don't know. Like everything else in life...I'll have to figure it out.

PAGES

TOM. *(Scribbles on a piece of paper he pulled from a pocket.)*
Here. Here's the directions.
(Hands the paper to **LEXI**.*)*
I'll be back in town next week. It might be the last time in a long while. My stockpile of gasoline is running awfully low. I've been able to become self-sustaining. If you want, I can pick you up and whatever stuff you need and move you out to my place.
(Hesitates, then continues.)
There are a few small houses on my property. We could each have our own space.

PETER. *(interrupting)*
You have room for me too?

*(***ALEX** *approaches)*

TOM. Of course. That's why I was telling you guys. Can you be ready in a week?

ALEX. Ready for what? Sorry I'm late.

LEXI. Alex! You made it!

*(***ALL** *greet with hugs.)*

TOM. I was just offering to let them come live with me.

ALEX. Oh?

TOM. You could come, too.

ALEX. No, I couldn't. I still have too many things I need to do here…for the library.

PAGES

PETER. Alex, we've done all we can for the library. I think you should consider it. Life isn't getting any easier here.

ALEX. I know that. That's exactly why I have to stay. At least for a while. In fact, I almost didn't come here tonight.

LEXI. Why? It was your idea to meet this day at this time.

ALEX. Yeah, but, remember how I thought I was being watched?

(**ALL** *nod*)

ALEX. It was true. I was being watched. But not by the authorities, like I thought.

LEXI. Who, then?

ALEX. *(Looks around for a moment before continuing.)* People from a town about a hundred miles away. Somehow they heard about what we did, and found a way to contact me. I've been helping them salvage the remnants of their library. It's gone now, too. We set up a code to get messages to each other, and we've contacted a few other groups in cities across the region.

LEXI. So we aren't the only ones doing this?

ALEX. It's surprising how many people have been involved in similar endeavors. Some started before we did, but most of them heard what happened to my mom, and decided it was time to take the risk and save their libraries in her honor.

TOM. Wow.

PAGES

PETER. That's fantastic.

ALEX. We've been trying to make records about what volumes we've been able to save. It hasn't been easy because we can't send any electronic documents or trust the mail. We can't take the chance that they might fall into the wrong hands, so it's all being done by hand, with pen and paper…and you know how hard it is to find that these days.

TOM. Are there no computerized records?

ALEX. Like I said, too hard to keep away from the internet eyes.

TOM. If there's a way to get these lists to me…I could create a master database. Like I was telling Lexi and Peter, I've been off the grid for years, now. I have systems in place from recording my own collection.

ALEX. That's a great idea. Thanks. I'll let the others know next time I see them. It will take time, since we can't use phones or internet, but I think I can start gathering lists in a few months. *(Beat)* A couple of years at the most. Where can I find you?

TOM. Lexi, you won't need those directions, right? Since I'm picking you up?

LEXI . Right. Here, Alex,
(hands paper to ALEX*)*
you keep this.

ALEX. *(Looking at paper)*
I know this place. It's perfect. How about this? Since you're so close, why don't you meet me in two years…at the book safe

house? I'll gather more computers by then and we can get a system set up.

TOM. Sounds perfect. If you need me to do anything before then, you can get a message to me there.

(Indicates paper)

LEXI. Me too, since I'll be staying there, too.

PETER. Count me in, too. If you're sure, Tom, that you have room.

TOM. Of course I have room. I'll pick you guys up in a week.

LEXI. *(Nods)*

PETER. I can't leave that soon.

TOM. How soon can you be ready? We need to settle details now. I can make a few more trips, but then gas will be a problem. Lexi, is a week good for you?

LEXI. *(Nods)*
I can be ready by then.

TOM. *(Thoughtfully)*
You know, it might be best to make different trips anyway. That way you can each bring more of whatever you'll need.

PETER. Three weeks…will that be ok?

TOM. Sure. I'll get you three weeks from today.

PAGES

ALEX. I have to cut this short. People are waiting for me. See you in two years, or maybe sooner, but two years, for sure.

TOM. For sure.

LEXI. Bye.

PETER. Stay safe. I have to go, too.

(**ALL** *embrace, then go their separate ways.*)

NARRATOR. Everyone was concerned about the collapse of the economy, and the devastation left in the wake of increasingly violent weather and man's destruction of the environment. However, there was another…larger…problem lurking just out of sight. Scientists tried to warn everyone, the government, the public…everyone…about the risks of solar storms, about their potential to disrupt…and possibly destroy…a vital part of society.

Unfortunately, no one paid much attention. There had been too many doomsday predictions throughout history, Nostradamus, Y2K, the end of the Mayan calendar in 2012. Solar storms were brushed off like just another prophecy destined to disappoint. That is if you can call "failure to destroy life as we know it" a disappointment.

Solar flares produce increased magnetic fields. Historically, they've been responsible for failures in satellite-based technology. Did you ever have your television go all weird even when it wasn't raining? It could have been from a solar flare. They happen all the time.

But…

PAGES

This time, the flares were far more powerful than any that had been previously recorded. The majority of earth's satellites were destroyed. Power grids were affected to the point of causing widespread black outs.

In some cities, electricity was not restored for months.

All satellite communication ceased. That meant no more television, no internet, no GPS, no radar to predict storms, and no cell phone service.

It was a time of great darkness.

PAGES

Scene 7

Several years later.

NARRATOR/ALEX and **ALEX** *walk to center stage,* **ALEX** *hands off the "identifying" lanyard/tie to* **NARRATOR/ALEX**. **ALEX** *exits.*

NARRATOR/ALEX. Yes, the future looked dismally bleak. But even in the darkest of times, a light will shine through, bringing hope thanks to those willing to make a difference.

*(***TOM, LEXI***,* **PETER** *enter and approach* **NARRATOR/ALEX***.)*

NARRATOR/ALEX. It's good to see you all.

TOM. Have you heard any more news from any of the other groups?

NARRATOR/ALEX. I did in fact. I heard from a group from Western Pennsylvania. Their Amish neighbors have been helping them learn to live the old fashioned way, in exchange for use of their library. They've been bartering for services, farm equipment, and horses.

PETER. That's great. We've been working on wind and solar powered generators. While we can't supply everyone, we have been able to produce enough for our homes.

LEXI. And we're here to get one installed to run the computers.

TOM. Once it's up and running, you'll be better able to function.

LEXI. I think it's amazing how we were able to get this set up. It looks like libraries used to look. We never could have done this without you, Alex.

PAGES

NARRATOR/ALEX. And I never would have been motivated to go so far with the whole thing if Mom and Libby hadn't given their lives to get it started. Do you think they realized how important their plan to save a few books really was?

TOM. I doubt anyone could have guessed that things would get as ugly as they did.

PETER. Or that the world would have taken so many weird twists and turns.

LEXI. You know something? I just thought of this.

NARRATOR/ALEX. What?

LEXI. Back when I was a kid, and your mom showed me how to use the library...
(Pause)

NARRATOR/ALEX. Yeah? Go on...what?

LEXI. The first thing she helped me research was the very first library...the one started in Alexandria. How fitting is it that you, Alex, are in charge of the first library in these times.

(Lights fade out.)

The End

ABOUT THE CHARACTER NAMES

ALEX – Named for the birthplace of all libraries "Alexandria."

LEXI – Named for "Lexicon" meaning "all of the words in a language" or dictionary.

LIBBY – Named for a variation of the Spanish word for book – *libro*.

PAIGE – Represents either a page of a book, or a type of library employee.

PETER – Named after Peter Ustinov who played the role of an elderly man in the abandoned library in the movie *Logan's Run*.

TOM – Represents a variation of the word "tome" which is another word for a book.

ABOUT THE AUTHOR

Debra R. Sanchez has moved over thirty times...so far. She and her husband have three adult children, four grandchildren, as well as a cat and a dog. She leads and attends various writing groups in the Pittsburgh area and also hosts writing retreats. Her writing has won awards at writers conferences in various genres, including children's stories, poetry, fantasy, fiction, and creative nonfiction. Several of her plays and monologues have been produced and published. Her other works have been published in literary magazines, newspapers, and anthologies.

For more information, visit her webpage:
www.DebraRSanchez.com

Follow her on Facebook: @DebraRSanchez

and Twitter: @DebraRSanchez